KNEE-DEEP
IN BLAZING SNOW

Knee-Deep in Blazing Snow

Growing Up in Vermont

Poems by James Hayford
Chosen by X. J. Kennedy & Dorothy M. Kennedy

Illustrations by Michael McCurdy

WORDSONG

These poems come from three collections by James Hayford: *Star in the Shed Window: Collected Poems 1933–1988* (The New England Press, Shelburne, Vermont, 1989), *Uphill Home* (The New England Press, 1992), and *Notes Left Behind: Last and Selected Poems* (1997). The latter book and the autobiography *Recollecting Who I Was* (2003), from which factual information has been drawn, are published by Oriole Books (distributed by James Hayford, Jr., West Road, Burlington, Vermont 05401).

Thanks to the people who made this book possible, especially Helen Hayford; James Hayford, Jr.; Don Craig; Howard Frank Mosher; Garret Keizer; and Paul D. Eschholz, publisher, The New England Press. Some facts in our introduction and in the biography of James Hayford come from Garret Keizer's article "Yankee Rebel" (*Vermont Life*, Winter 1989); Howard Frank Mosher's "Letter from Vermont" (*Book World*, August 10, 1986); and Sally Pollak's feature article in the *Burlington Free Press* (December 26, 1999).

LIBRARY OF CONGRESS CATALOGING-IN-PUBLICATION DATA
Hayford, James.
Knee-deep in blazing snow: growing up in Vermont: poems by James Hayford;
chosen by X. J. Kennedy & Dorothy M. Kennedy;
illustrated by Michael McCurdy.
p. cm.
ISBN 1-59078-338-7 (alk. paper)
1. Vermont—Juvenile poetry.
2. Children's poetry, American.
I. Kennedy, X. J. II. Kennedy, Dorothy M. III. McCurdy, Michael. IV. Title.

PS3558.A84K58 2005
811'.54-dc22
2004030658

Published by Wordsong
Boyds Mills Press, Inc
A Highlights Company

KNEE-DEEP
IN BLAZING SNOW

Contents

Contents

James Hayford's World
an introduction

Jumping into piles of hay. Watching a newborn lamb totter to its feet. Hearing the drumbeat of maple trees dropping sap into pails. The joy of pulling on socks dried on a hot radiator. Here is a world far from the honking cars and fast life of big cities. It is James Hayford's Vermont world.

In the Northeastern village of Orleans where he last lived, Hayford was well known. People would see him walking along, sometimes stopping and thinking, maybe writing a poem in his head. At first, Hayford published his poems himself in little books sold at craft fairs. His poems became well loved by many people in Vermont. People cut them out and carried them in their wallets, or posted them on their refrigerators. "He's the wisest person I've ever met," said his friend Howard Frank Mosher. "Jim is a great man in the way you'd want your president to be."

Tucked in a valley between the Green Mountains and the White Mountains, James Hayford's world has startling seasons. Fall is a blaze of color. Then the world becomes an icebox for half a year. The coming of spring is a joyful event. Summer, while green and beautiful, may be too brief to ripen a tomato. A summer visitor once told an old farmer, "You're lucky to live in Vermont! I'd move here too, if only the winters weren't so terrible!" "Yep," said the old man, "if it wasn't for the winters, everybody'd move to Vermont."

In Hayford's poems, you'll hear that Vermont way of talking—with no wasted words. The poems tend to be short, and they are always carefully made, as if carved by hand. Poems don't always need to rhyme, but you'll find that Hayford favors rhyming. Writing a poem, he once said, is a matter of placing words exactly, as a mason places bricks: "Rhyme keeps our corners firm."

To get the most fun from his poems, read them aloud, slowly. James Hayford wrote for everybody, not only kids; but he hoped young people would enjoy his poems. Out of 774 poems he left, here are some we hope you will like, and maybe try learning by heart.
—*X. J. K. and D. M. K.*

SUMMER

Hay-Jumpers

When hay was put in loose,
We jumpers had our use:
We packed the stuff away.

Climbing the side of the bay
To a high ledge, we'd stand,
Each pick his place to land,
Then soar off into space
And plunge up to his face
In the sweet springy stuff.

By noon we'd had enough.
The jumping was pure play
But breathing chaff in the murk
Was quite a lot like work
On a blue-and-gold hay day.

Barn Swallow

Your barn swallow is a born barnstormer,
A daredevil of a performer:
See him mount almost out of sight
And, taking passage on a draft,
Slip forward, sideways, even aft,
Then skim the grass but never light,
And once more climb—
He must be having a high time—
I would, if I had his air craft.

Egg in the Pocket

Go pocket a fresh egg
And then go bump that leg
Next time you come to turn

A corner in the barn;

Maybe someday you'll learn
What not to leave to chance—
Including nice dry pants.

The Skunk

You talk about imagination—think:
A creature armed with nothing but a stink
Propelled to make aggressors stop and blink.

About his bad name as a dirty fighter,
Compared, say, to a scratcher or a biter,
You have to ask what makes it so much righter

To kill an enemy than make him cough
Just long enough so you can get clean off.

Between Trains

This railroad bridge I use
Most times I walk to town
Is empty between trains.

If I had any brains
I'd pick some place to clown
Where there'd be less to lose.

Two Birds (With One Stone)

1

No wonder *grackle*'s a sad word—
The grackle's a sad bird:

He hasn't any song, he squawks;
He has no hop, he flatly walks.

Ill-tempered too, he drives away
Nice birds who'd like to stay.

Unfortunate his whole design—
Nothing about him you'd call fine.

How burdensome to be a bird
For whom nobody has a good word!

2

At the opposite pole
Is the oriole

Of golden throat
And golden note

And golden name.
Is he to blame

For taking what
No grackle's got?

Why, that's your duty
If born a beauty.

The Mirror of My Realm

In the corner back beyond,
Where the brook enters the spruces,
I have a little pond;
Its banks are smoothly lawned
And it has several uses.

The cattle come to drink,
A frog lives in the brink,
It is my swimming pool;
I take there what I think
Is the only sport that's cool.

On the cool grass I sit
At dusk and look at it,
Composing clouds and the elm
That rises opposite—
The mirror of my realm.

It takes far things and tall
And lays them at my feet
While sleepy thrushes call.
I haven't to leave my seat
To have my world complete.

On His Side of the River

A dog that chases cars
Is an ill-mannered cur,
And I don't know any cure.

One dog, at a place I pass,
Has found a way to give chase
Without even coming close:

A river wide though shallow
Divides this clever fellow
From the cars he aims to follow,

And I say, Good dog, Rover;
Chase back and forth forever—
On your side of the river.

What It Took to Win

As a boy I never won a single fight.
I started some when shoved or called a sissy,
And tried to finish plenty when hit first.
I wasn't afraid of hitting or getting hit,
But never quite had what it took to win.
"Say uncle!" "Uncle," I'd say, and homeward march,
Mad all over at the rotten system
And the unbeatable, by me, world.

Goats in Pasture

Their bony heads untaxed by need of moving,
Changing, repairing, laying by,
Goats keep a comprehensive eye
On the condition of the sky—
Such store they set on keeping dry—
And live attentively, without improving.

Approaching Thunder

Shh! Up the valley I hear thunder.
The afternoon's turned hushed and black.
Twilight at four is such a wonder.
Perhaps we'd better be getting back.

See—up the valley there, it's raining.
Smell it already—that green smell.

The robins feel it coming, gaining—
They shout let it come on, pell-mell.

Oh, that cool breath will blow it nearer.
Flash—that was close—and closer yet.
Each leaf turns up a flashing mirror.
Splash! Get inside or you'll get wet.

The Mystery of Day

I've hunted everywhere inside
Where anything might try to hide:

Behind the doors and taller chairs
And underneath the beds upstairs;

In a closet dense with dangling belts
I heard a chuckle somewhere else;

On tiptoe, fingering the wall,
I heard a footfall in the hall;

I turned the knob and let it squeak—
The hall was empty, bright and bleak.

The mystery of day all right
Is how its shades keep out of sight.

Call It a Day

I used to hate to call it a day
On summer eves when put to bed
With all that molten light out there
And the older kids still playing in it.

FALL

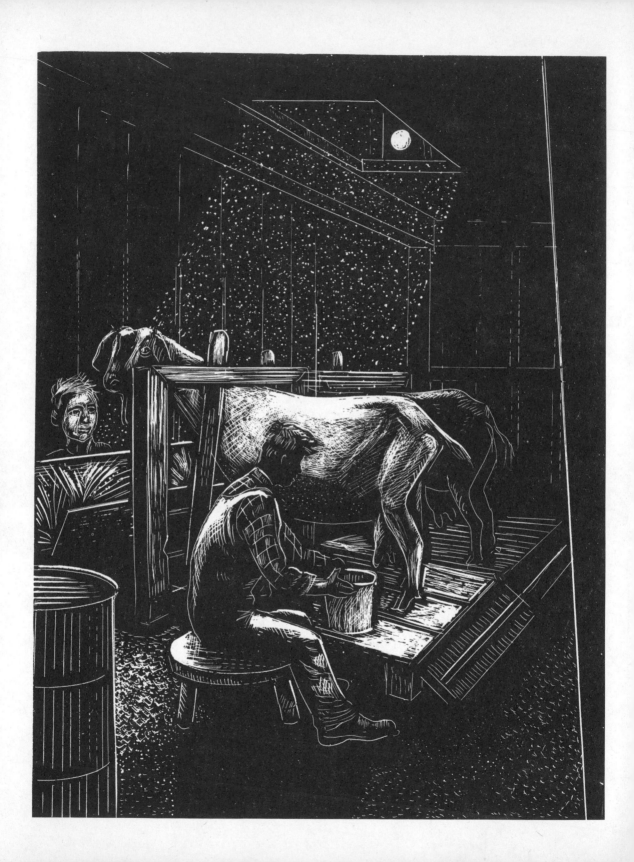

Night Milking Time

Night milking time in our goat barn
With hand-hewn frame and planking worn
From daily passing, night and morn;

Across the board wall, mellowed brown,
Light from the windowed loft slants down
Through the trapdoor where hay is thrown;

The dusky stable facing east
Rumbles with many a munching beast,
Smelling of out-of-doors, snow-fleeced.

How low in light of all the sky
The space here covered dim and dry—
And yet so generous, so high,

One tenant more would cause no cramp
If I should make a corner-camp
In here tonight—no bed, no lamp.

Night Windows

Night windows that you pass
On after-supper tramps
Afford you such a glimpse
Of chairbacks and pale lamps
So close beyond the glass

That once in every street
You almost think you're meant
To see what they have to eat
And what they burn for heat,
And how they are content.

Early to Bed

Early to bed
Leaves dark ahead

In which to wake
As by mistake

And hear the train
Approach and wane—

And sleep again.

Widower's Windows

Old widower saves lights
By supping early, nights,

Wipes his two dishes dry
By the last light of the sky,

Rocks some time in the dark
To settle his beans and pork,

Then feels his way to bed
Where stars attend his head.

Shower on the House

It knocks on the roof with liquid knuckles,
Envelops the porch in gutteral chuckles,
Cascades in white sheets off the flashing,
Scatters itself with its own splashing.

Moonset

Moon down at the end of Main Street
Where the land westward drops
To sidings where the trains meet,

How close you stand to stare
Into deserted shops
Around the vacant square.

WINTER

First Snow

Blanketing fields that lately were bare brown,
Let this soft midnight snow bring blessings down
On all the people in the little town.

Wet Socks

Nothing I own
Is sure to improve with time
Like these wet socks
On the radiator
That I'll put on
Dry and warm
Later.

Love of Snow

In those years, days like this
When the storm made the oak leaves hiss
Were days of winter bliss:

Pulling our sleds to the top
Of town where houses stop
And fields and pastures drop

Over back to farms and the river,
We'd slide and climb forever—
Till first dark made us shiver;

Then homeward tired and slow,
Ready for kitchen glow,
All white from love of snow.

The Cardinal

The cardinal must know he shows
In winter woods all white and black;

He must see all the world as foes
And all day long expect attack.

Despite the cardinal's success,
I try for inconspicuousness.

The Poor

We see them keeping warm
Before and after storm
As prisoners to whom
The world assigns one room,
Its door and window cracks
Stoppered with burlap sacks—

We see them meanly holed
Up, rags all helter-skelter
In shells that aren't much shelter
At twenty-five below
Against the cleanly cold,
The glittering stars and snow.

Trains

That southbound train at dawn
Took its first travelers on,
Starting in dark somewhere;

This northbound at twilight
Is heading into night,
And someone's going there.

Barn Light

Barn light on the blank snow
Assures me as I go
No time could be more proper:

Cattle are being fed,
No one has gone to bed—
I shall be home for supper.

The Busy Town

At sundown then my mother and I
Walked with the wind along the street;
The sky was red in front of us,
The cold snow creaked beneath our feet.

When we at last arrived downtown
Some people talked with us and I
Looked into lighted windows full
Of clocks and rugs and toys to buy.

Too soon we turned back to the long
Dark street and faced into the wind;
Someone creaked past us, hurrying down
To join the throng before it thinned.

January Night

The shiny trodden snow
In harsh illumination,
So cold your boot soles creak;
The houses double-glassed
Against the searching blast—
These things you may have classed
Under the heading, Bleak.

Fact is, the snow was trod
By people warmly shod
And coated—none in mink—
Sashaying to and fro
Betwixt the stores, the station,
Tavern, and house of God,
And this bright, crowded rink.

SPRING

Spring Tide

Of signs that spring is come,
One, less remarked than some,
Is the multiple dull drum

Of sap in empty pails.
Noons when the sun prevails
Over late March's gales,

Along the streaming roads
In mountain neighborhoods
You come on sugar woods

Knee-deep in blazing snow
Where pails drum high, drum low,
With this sweet tidal flow.

The Banished Cat

Dear cat who slept between our feet,
Now banished from the electric sheet,
We miss your little body curled
Beside us in the dark of the world.

Time to Plant Trees

Time to plant trees is when you're young
So you will have them to walk among—

So, aging, you can walk in shade
That you and time together made.

The Tractor

Printing a dented track
Over the rolling meadow
As it putts forth and back
In the little leaves' light shadow—

Free as toy wheels print roads
In the dirt by the kitchen door—
It rambles with many loads
At large on the land once more.

Feeding Time

Our new lamb loves the feel
Of legs and back and tail:
See her fling up a heel
Advancing to the pail.

A Robin's Work

By eight a robin's morning's work
Is already half done
Since he began at four o'clock
Before the sun.

How many worms must one unearth
To do a robin's-worth?

Paleface

How pale my back and sides
Compared to horses' hides
Which may be black or bay,
Roan, chestnut, dapple-gray . . .
If asked I would have voted
To be as richly coated.

The Wash

Already on the line
Sunning and well astir,
The wash'll be dry by nine
Or earlier.

The catbird in the bush
Is helping things along;
He gives the air a push
With his mad song.

Pasture Puddles

Days when the pasture land
In rain lets the white sky
Into the watery ground,
I step where heavens lie
Below me all around.

Rain on the Roof

A light rain overhead,
And under it, abed,
Sheltered and comforted,
We fell asleep to the patter
Of softly falling water.

About James Hayford

James Hayford (1913–1993) lived in Vermont for almost his whole life. He was born in Montpelier, the smallest state capital in the country. His father hoped he would be an athlete, but the boy couldn't see well enough: he had to start wearing glasses when he was three. Early, he began to study music and at age twelve was already a church organist.

When he went to Amherst College, he studied with the famous poet Robert Frost. Frost took an interest in the young man and offered him a bargain. Hayford would receive one thousand dollars—enough, back in 1935, to live on for a whole year—if he would promise to remain in America, keep away from advanced studies, and devote himself to writing poems.

Hayford kept the spirit of the bargain. After a short time teaching in New Jersey, he returned to Vermont, living mostly in the northeastern villages of West Burke and Orleans. He and his wife, Helen, raised a son, also named James, and had grandchildren. Most of the time, Hayford earned a living by teaching English, history, and music, but sometimes he raised goats, grew raspberries, drove a taxi, worked as a helper to a carpenter, and directed church choirs.

All the while, Hayford kept writing. Some of his poems appeared in national magazines such as *Harper's, The New Yorker,* and *The Saturday Evening Post.* But many years went by until, when he was seventy-three, his books at last found a professional publisher. His *Gridley Firing,* illustrated by Mary Azarian, is a children's story about a skunk who helps a family save their farm from a greedy developer (Shelburne, Vermont: New England Press, 1987). Soon after, the same publisher brought out two books of poetry: *Star in the Shed Window: Collected Poems* (1989) and *Uphill Home* (1992).

Late in his life, Hayford's poems began to win more readers. Lee Bennett Hopkins and other anthologists included some of them in children's books. Weeks before James Hayford died, the University of Vermont honored him with the degree of Doctor of Humane Letters. *Notes Left Behind* (Burlington: Oriole Books, 1997) brings together his last poems and a selection from his earlier works.

Robert Frost made a wise investment. James Hayford's poetry will endure and continue to find new admirers far beyond the boundaries of New England.

Photo by Jamie Cope

About Michael McCurdy

Michael McCurdy, widely recognized for his work in woodcut and scratchboard, began his career as a book artist in 1963. Currently, 177 books contain his art. As an author as well as an illustrator, his books for children include *An Algonquian Year* (Houghton Mifflin), *Trapped by Ice! Shackleton's Amazing Antarctic Adventure* (Walker), and *Hannah's Farm: The Seasons on an Early American Homestead* (Holiday House). In December 2000, three of his illustrated books were chosen for *Yankee Magazine's* list of the 100 best books ever written about life in New England, and one of them, *Giants in the Land,* was selected for the magazine's list of a "top 40." McCurdy attended the School of the Museum of Fine Arts in Boston, where he later taught, and Tufts University. For seventeen years, his *Penmaen Press* produced finely printed limited first editions by many notable writers. He and his wife, Deborah, now live in the Berkshires of Massachusetts. They have two grown children.

About X. J. and Dorothy M. Kennedy

The Kennedys have collaborated on two best-selling poetry anthologies for children, both from Little, Brown: *Talking Like the Rain* (1992) and *Knock at a Star: A Child's Introduction to Poetry* (1982; revised edition, 1999). X. J. Kennedy, whose poems for adults have earned several awards and three honorary degrees, is the author of fourteen children's books, including *Elympics* (Philomel) and a novel *The Eagle as Wide as the World* (Margaret K. McElderry Books). He is the year 2000 recipient of the NCTE Award for Excellence in Children's Poetry. More than three million college students have used his textbooks, including *An Introduction to Poetry, Ninth Edition.* Dorothy M. Kennedy has collaborated on two of these textbooks, and on her own is the author of two poetry anthologies for children, *Make Things Fly* (McElderry) and *I Thought I'd Take My Rat to School* (Little, Brown). In spring 2000 she contributed a round-up article on poetry anthologies for the bulletin of the Children's Book Council. The parents of five grown children, the Kennedys live in Lexington, Massachusetts.